1

Monozygotic | Codependent

by
Stephanie Bryant Anderson

Monozygotic | Codependent

Published by Blue Hour Press, May 2015
McMinnville Oregon, USA

thebluehourmagazine.com

Printed in the USA

Book Design: Susan Sweetland Garay & Moriah
        LaChapell
Cover Photo: Tom Gorman
Cover Design: Susan Sweetland Garay & Moriah
        LaChapell
Edited by: Susan Sweetland Garay, Moriah
        LaChapell & Heather Minette
ISBN 10 – 0989013782
ISBN 13 - 978-0-9890137-8-9

I do not know who I am, where I am going - and I am the one who has to decide the answers to these hideous questions.

—Sylvia Plath

Loneliness Came Inside My Home, Unpacked Its Things

I sat on the floor
in a blue room choking

on emotions, confessing
sadness to the cake falling

down my throat, wondering
how I have come to hate winter

when it snows
such beautiful white flowers.

But—

it's the way I've neatly folded the laundry
over and over.

It's the way fear visits me twice,
and courage once.

It's the way I move alone at night
from the couch to the door

to the curtains,
back to the couch.

It's how you catch me dreaming
and step over my body.

For Charlcie—

who is 6 minutes older.

TABLE OF CONTENTS

9. Loneliness Came Inside My Home, Unpacked Its Things
17. Don't put all your eggs in one basket
19. The Generation Dress
22. Waiting on Mother
24. Before My Sister Boarded the Plane for Paris I Bit Her
25. In the hours that you're gone
26. Reflection in the Dance Studio Mirror
28. Between the silences there are sounds like panic
30. Take Down the Clouds
31. Regret
32. Married Women, and other degenerates
33. Like the Black Hole Cartographer Who Went Hunting for Walnuts
34. Dirt
35. The Hanging Field
36. Bertha Mason is a Fictional Character
38. Leftovers
39. After Jake's Funeral
41. Anxiety While Crossing the Tennessee-Arkansas Bridge
42. When Joe Proposed
43. Staring at a Dead Bird in a Wendy's Parking Lot
45. Into the Icy Field Again
46. Signing Divorce Papers

47. Co dependence
48. Broken Egg
49. A Letter to My Divorce
51. He carries me in the biology of his body
53. The Kitchen Fire, 2013
55. Barriers
57. The Funeral Procession is for Saying Goodbye
58. My God, While Rummaging Through the Attic
60. Apartment J-82
62. The Poem for Evelyn
64. Why Death recalls more Lovers and Cats than the Moon (or why I am the lonely Cat Lady up talking to God at 4 a.m.)
66. Sometimes I Pack my Things and Leave

Don't put all your eggs in one basket

But, my mother did—

the first time she put in an egg in the form
of a prayer, *God is a wide open door*,

and with her bird-throat asked
God for food.

The next day in the driveway, the violent
blows of February long gone—a ten dollar bill.

Now provided for, Mother ate bread
and white beans, while outside rain

fell in the language of apologies.
When spring returned birds

to nests ceremoniously decorated
in the eaves of the porch with gooseberries

and the tab of an aluminum can, Mother
put two more eggs in her basket, this time,

giving them names. As they hatched
she said, *I'm gonna have twins, too.*

17

Because—it's my turn.

The doctor, hearing only one heartbeat,
didn't listen hard enough—

God is waiting from the tops of tin roofs
overlooking a sky of birds' feet, and a horse,

a withered field, and yellow-brown water standing
in the yard.

For three generations two children nested
in the wombs of our mothers

like small eggs waiting to be found
in the high grass.

The Generation Dress

They shaped the dress material like a shoulder;
Maw, Memaw, Mother, mussed
out a design still empty
of its spine, while I, who made four,
slipped my arm in. I wanted to switch
the angles, make the dress into what I wanted.

                    The oldest
smelled like winter's snow, and shuffled
to and from her sewing kit like Germany
in her polyester clothes. With her glasses
slipping from her nose, she cut the peach
fabric to mimic the thin, flimsy pattern,
and grew my chin out of her wooden boat. Maw
ironed the pieces down, hummed
in unison with the steam. She was a magician woman
born with silver-fox hair that she wore long & loose.

Her ass pressed against her daughter,
whose hair is dark like mine; Memaw
stooped at my feet taking measurements,
a beauty born in late Fall; she could make
the moon fall even still with her crooked fingers.
September 1976 when I crouched

from below the Earth's spine,
the first time I saw her, I knew love.

The hem's needles scratched at my legs,
when I tried the skirt on, clawed like *die katze*:
miau!miau! she screeched through the needles
clutched in her teeth.

The third is up and down,
her moods like a slipped zipper.
She wore green like a sea monster,
and made love to her husband
when he wasn't home. Though Mother cooked
out of boxes, her scissors cut well.

The pieces of dress grew together,
my shoulders and neck, the bodice and pleats,
creating the shape of a woman. The shape I did not yet
have.

When I grew into a woman, I wanted
legs and an ass thinner
than their legs and asses,
perkier breasts than their baby sucked breasts,
and smaller hips.

As they finished,

I stared at photographs of twins on Memaw's walls
my uncles;
my great aunts;
my sister and I, all identical;
and with cooked eggs falling from my mouth,
I tried the dress on—

Waiting on Mother

From the screen door I can see
the dim light

of the living room and her silence
digging into the roots

of the dogwood tree as the sun
goes down.

I am waiting for my mother. I am
alone on a porch

that still burns my legs like the dream
that burns my chest.

I hear the clink of her glass against
the cluttered end table.

She is eating a popcorn dinner alone.
For many years, while she grew as distant as stars,

my sisters and I
have grown into women.

She does not look up from the TV,

she is not lonely,
I think—

Before My Sister Boarded the Plane for Paris I Bit Her

As she left, I was afraid she would find Paris
a sweet place.

A noise of storm-water wailed in my head—
she might not come back.

In our birth,
Mother drew her to the surface first, marked her

Baby A. When she broke loose
I heard the womb spread, I saw

instruments and lenses. I became her shadow,
she, my four walls.

From Paris she sent a picture:
the bruise showed

a lockjaw of words, a map
back to me.

Without her, the world finds me a bore.
Without her, the mirror is only a reflection.

When she did come back, she said
every day it rained.

In the hours that you're gone

My sleeping bones live, like snow on snow,
I hear them speak: another day, another night.

Another. Another.
Sometimes
                    in the hours that you're gone
my blood goes cold.

Reflection in the Dance Studio Mirror

I want to be like you,
better than beautiful—but

in second position,
my thighs touch. I pull

my sweatshirt from my fat folds—
as if doing so makes me thin.

The other dancers never saw how
the Miss Piggy hoodie fit too tight,

or the way my legs squeezed into
the matching pink pants.

My reflection cowers,
like a disgraced animal. She says

Tchaikovsky and other boys
will never want me.

I study my outline closely, Mother's voice
cracking in my head:

you should hope to grow tall,
and *don't wear thick sweaters.*

Needing to get back to dancing,
my chest spreads open.

Do you understand now—
how my voice never developed?

Between the silences there are sounds like panic

The Statler Brothers are singing a golden song
while we eat our eggs sunny side up.

My sister whispers in my ear: *Do you remember
the sound the door made when he locked you in?*

The memory floods like burning urine floods
the bladder;

I empty the lemonade from a plastic teacup—
my nausea excited at the way my uncle eats

breakfast breathing through his mouth, smiling at
the plate

while he breaks the thin layer of skin
to open the yolks.

Grandmother hangs her hair over the kitchen sink,
colors over her gray with the color of ripe

lemons—covering over all the dreadful things—
the daisy wallpaper peels

where she tried to hide the way the wood-burning
stove turned the walls canary.

28

She washes a pear even though it has bruised
to near inedible.

A sunbeam tries to lighten my hair, but my hair
refuses to let go its crow feathers—

hair the color of the night, the same night
that beyond my bedroom window

let in the yellow rapeseed.

Take Down the Clouds

When I almost drowned while swimming, your tentacled
arms covered me in scales—a pattern

of movement sequences repeated—and you returned me,
the drowned girl from water—my purplish skin

a wild iris wilting. I un-swallowed the vodka, and you
pushed the clouds back over the romantic moon

and argued that mermaids do not live inside of every sad
woman. Your belief in universal design

says I am the lungs. And you, the inseparable
breath moving through to keep me alive.

I saw you in the sky—Spica—my binary star—
the brightest star in Virgo. Even in mother-water,

you didn't leave me, you pulled me along, giving me
constellations and harmonies to live in,

and touched my toes to the bottom of the pool.
You've never let me slip away—

my body smooth as a pearl.

Regret

You lay your quick horses in my lap;
I think of how I would rather sleep,

but I say nothing out loud—I don't believe
in being pretty anymore,

or know why
I watch you read in bed.

We are simple,
there is nothing between us,

we are merely skin
and nothing more.

I shift my head,
see the complements of the lamp's shine

strong against the light and dark of your face—
I want to lay against your back

and urge your horses to gallop.
Instead, I turn my back to you.

I want to be beautiful,
but I say nothing aloud—

Married Women, and other degenerates

Standing at the screen door, the clouds
resemble pirate ships

searching for port—the rain weary and tired.
I wonder why they want the cold of earth.

He knows how to make rain a dirty word.
Vibrate it against skin.

Silent and alone, I sip tea. A glimpse of sunlight
hits my bone-cage. In an exhale, I untie my hair.

He said *wife*, and my bones scattered like snow
across the ground, like bombs and body parts.

Tracing the rowboat flooded across Ghost Bridge,
I motion to him like the red-birds flying past.

Watching the thin horizon line that ends one day
and begins another, I rest my head.

I knew better.

As he left, the screen door cut his foot.
He would be back for the flesh left in its metal.

Like the Black Hole Cartographer Who Went Hunting for Walnuts

When the door closed this time, she knew it
      would be different. She saw his eyes—
emotionless ticks that had grown into the plural

patterns of empty walnut shells. Someone once
      star-mapped Aries the Ram, and generously
gave him horns. *I am strong as an Ox*—

he reminded her as she stood to leave. Reminded
      her that she was the Year of the Rabbit with closed
curtains.

Safety over risk, she recalled looking at the door,
      but her body lied, it could not carry her there.
You cry too easily— he said, after the first hit

into her eye-bone crunched, sounding the way
      the nutcracker sounded when breaking open
walnuts. He stood over her

using the same angle God used to look down from.
       But, here, for her,
there was no longer a down—

Dirt

He planted my cat in the side yard.
Vines and bluegrass grew into her little ears.

A horse, two parakeets in a puzzle box, a family
of rabbits, and a dog or two lay in the hill next to her.

He took me to the side of the house, propped
the shovel against the siding and kissed me.

His mouth tasted like dirt after just burying
another dead thing.

As a child, I was told if I kept digging further
into holes,

I could dig my way to China.
He said once that I could do that,

dig and come through on the other side
like a beautiful flower.

The ground is already full of too many corpses—
I say.

The Hanging Field

Though we never stopped, we stared
from the backseat of our car—

our flat-bottom boat—at the body darting
from the end of a rope. I remember the road,

its lines, yellow and broken, the crowd
and a cloud shaped like a hare.

Now the field comes back into view:

I've dreamt a horse into the field, or the horse
in my dream came to save me—not

some knight—but the horse,
and I climbed onto his back to keep from

suffocating. But it was more than that—
I was trying to suffocate myself & this crazy

beautiful horse came running into the field
and his wild body kept me from hanging.

In the sky the scent of tobacco paraded,
and the magpies flew their black kites.

Bertha Mason is a Fictional Character

> —when you are by yourself; for if you don't repent,
> something bad might be permitted to come down the
> chimney, and fetch you away.
> *Jane Eyre*, Charlotte Bronte

I know how to hide things.
I hid the burns on my hands

from the oven's
child cakes, brownies,

whatever desserts didn't need
real baking.

I used to pretend I was Dumbo.
I learned elephants are scared of mice.

Someone said fat girls, like elephants,
should also be afraid—

and I hid away
while I ate. Icing.

Chocolate chip cookie dough.
Candy bars I bought from Circle K,

sure to hide the wrappers.
I am trying to take up enough space

so that someone will notice me.

I wait by the chimney
for the ghosts to come. Or even death.

My toes are cold. I worry
they are cold from poor circulation.

Paranoia. Or hope that someone
is set to arrive. Maybe I will start a fire—

Leftovers

You place the box of General Tso's in the fridge,
knowing you'll never go back to it, just as you

should have never brought home Mark again.
Still, you asked the waitress to box it up, accepting

that neglect is your method of cleanup.
You spend nights without much appetite

as you watch *The Late Show*
in your blue-shadowed living room, listening

to the laugh track you've come to mimic
in conversations with your coworkers and your cat.

Now, weeks later, reeking in the fridge,
the plastic take-home container smells of old lettuce

and rotting meat, and the stomach
of your memories spills

onto the floor in a big heap.

After Jake's Funeral

Will you not tell God if I bury death's bones
while no one is looking?

Will you not tell God that I refuse
to leave my dark-haired sister, my mirror girl?

Jake, at your funeral I sat alone
on a wooden pew, remembering

the way my sister and I
used to pick strawberries,

go to Slaughbach's to buy jam,
and take long drives every Sunday.

She gave me vegetables
from her garden: jalapeño peppers,

because she liked to teach me
Spanish.

You would not tell God that I just lied,
that we never did those things.

You would not tell God
I am standing outside her kitchen window

wanting in, waiting beside her husband
and her dog.

Jake, your brothers crashed to the floor
in front of your casket today.

Did you see the way they fell?

No—
you could not possibly tell God.

Anxiety While Crossing the Tennessee-Arkansas Bridge

Last November my sister got married.
My heart cropped, carried

for months in my handkerchief. At night
it would cry out from extinction.

This amputation being no small ache, I left
Tennessee, my heartbeat slow.

Memphis with her strange spell
filled my piano-ribs

with a slow blues loaded
with heavy bees and suicide ghosts.

The road tasted like salt. I drove until
I couldn't see the shape of us,

until my heart could again beat
on its own.

When Joe Proposed / the moon
looked like a broken bowl.

He stood waiting
with the patience of a sunrise—

I thought of another man.
The one that fed stray cats

in the *piazza*, the one who worried
when one would wander away.

We would stay awake
until hunger meant nothing,

until Italy slept in that soft spot
of morning, like leg on leg.

Before I could pretend
to make breakfast,

he thrust his hands into
his coat and left.

I said *yes* to Joe—my heart
shaped like the moon.

Staring at a Dead Bird in a Wendy's Parking Lot

I stood over it in the parking lot—deafened
at the dead bird whose wings shriveled

and tore like a thick cord of tobacco.
The eyes squeezed plum juice—rotten

fruit trapping the soul from coming or going,
though the brain so easily stopped.

The bird could do nothing. The neck, broken,
craned as if looking for someone

it didn't want to miss.

I recalled the night in the living room, when
my grandmother got out of bed

after taking her Ambien. She smiled sweetly
while watching The Miss America Pageant with us.

She went back to her room, grabbed a hand mirror.
Walking back in, she stared at her ass.

See, I am just as beautiful as they are—
I've still got it, girls!

Then dropping her nightgown to the ground, posed
as a nude contestant, her pubic hairs, wiry, shaped

like the dead bird—its legs up and frozen—
the sounds from the TV wild with laughter.

Into the Icy Field Again

Rows of corn keep snow from the road—
the long mound like a fresh grave.

How womanly the field guards herself, expecting
to keep the afterimage in her husks.

But—
the ground dutifully accepts grief.

Slipping down, the sun
knifes the day in half.

Afraid to sleep,
the smell of wet boots & blood fruit step in.

They come shaped as an open field plagued
by black irises—

an absorption of botany and anatomy.

In the field
a shadow fell like knees heavy to the ground.

I was a girl then. And now
my hands turn over and over inside themselves.

Signing Divorce Papers

The long drive from Tennessee took us
to the Travelodge in Gallup, New Mexico,

where we had sex to the sounds of bikers fighting
outside the door. Afterwards, he turned on

the TV, while I turned over to sleep.
A storm clung low in the desert,

its voice heavy and red. He used to tell me
his secrets, I believed.

When the clouds hit the mountain's plateau,
the storm died. He started

drinking coffee before bed,
while I slept alone.

We never fought,
not even as we divided our things:

the house, holidays, visitation, who will
mow the flat lawn, who will live alone.

Signing the papers, I remember in Gallup
the way the moon blinked from behind the darkness.

Co dependence

Beneath a thin sheet, I try to sleep—
the mouth of my curtains open.

Outside, frogs declare territory, croaking
from distant ponds. I dream of starry-eyed

geese angled in flight. After everyone has left
me, the house is too silent. On many nights,

I hear sirens from my bedroom, either from
an ambulance or fire-engine, screaming

like a scared woman.
I am never brave anymore.

Broken Egg

Losing warmth, my coat sleeve dangles
from the armchair. By the bed a cup of water

grows tepid while, like a watchdog,
medicine sleeps in me.

I wanted to study Russian
and brag of being a Mathematician;

instead, I hold tight to my cigarette—my hand
dangling in air

as if I were mid-sentence, or mid-thought,
but I think of nothing. The foggy moon,

and God's last round of sheep, resemble full ticks.
Shadows circle me as if hands on a clock—

the minutes steady blood ticking
in my veins. Morning is on its way,

the bird outside crying for sun.

A Letter to My Divorce

Forgive my legs
that burned with fireflies

while the snow died
from my knees.

I sat in silence in the kitchen chairs
that once filled with family.

Forgive that hum
that arrived in my throat

before summer
that now stutters like a tic,

clearing in conversations
on the phone.

And the flowers you left
without a note, and the way

I can't forgive how I
bowed my head in the black

stillness of early morning,

afraid to turn on the lights to see

you were not here.
Forgive these, too.

He carries me in the biology of his body

I wrap the uncooked lamb in white paper to place back
in the fridge. The blood weeps through.

I imagine the knife—a plunging warship. The cesarean
that cut him out of me. The anodyne.

Like an umbilical, the onion-shaped corpuscles
of my blood attach to him, fill him with my phantoms.

Before dinner I tell him, no candy. *Then—*
I am going to kill myself. With a knife.

And I will scare you. He believes the knife
will bring relief. The blood. The slowing heart.

At times, his eyes are small rooms whose lights are out.
A darkness that even the cold doesn't reach.

I have loved him from the inside. But
love alone does not help us.

Spoiling him, I gather him in the place where
our blood gathers, and put him in my bed to sleep.

We are drifting off—together.
I worry my blood is not warm enough—

The Kitchen Fire, 2013

The smoke grew dark as vulture wings.
It stayed on the ceiling as if taking

what was dead to feed its young—
the fire mouthing the cabinets.

I can tell you now, the way
the heat from the fire pressed itself

against my lungs. I tried to drag my grandmother
from the kitchen. Running out

the backdoor to take in fresh air,
I thought how life always happened

more outside than in. The Mennonite
greenhouse. The flowerbeds. The garden.

Her diamond earrings. Keeping appearances.
And now, on her ceiling, the vultures have

circled in every room, the charred smell

fetching us away. Her heart slowing.

Barriers

The brush rattles—
the way death sounds

in my grandmother's rattled
throat.

A doe and two fawn
walk by so close

that if I open the window
I could brush them

with my fingers. But—
I don't bother,

and the deer cross
the clearing.

Glass between us.
The small barrier

I press my forehead against.

In the morning, I know a hunter
will reach into the field,

and my grandmother's coffin
will hold her like a new dress.

The Funeral Procession is for Saying Goodbye

She has died, I say,
and my tongue goes numb.

I watch myself leave,
one ghost at a time:

the tin-voiced granddaughter,
quiet, protective, role

of mother. Someone,
who needs to understand grief,

telephones, but I cannot answer—
cannot make myself say goodbye.

Neither can my jaw, heavy,
refuse death's blue shape.

Slow as a clock's second hand,
the hearse, like a shiny black raincoat,

outlines the objects of my life; my shell,
all the beautiful travelers

who quickened my blood,
now gone.

My God, While Rummaging through the Attic
after Sandra Beasley

My god used to leave me love notes on the kitchen
table. *I've gone to the store—be back soon.*

She didn't want to wake me
or worry me, as she knew how I would hurt

thinking she was lost somewhere
between astronomy and agriculture.

But this time,
my god didn't come back.

When she comes to wander the house again
my god will ask why her clothes

from the back closet have gone missing.
I don't want to tell her we've lied to her.

Listening to the New Testament on vinyl,
my god will hum a song I don't know,

while I remove the dirt from her feet, her hands.
Everything here reminds me she has left—

like the red and white ceramic hen sitting
in a box.

My god used to pop off
its head and plant diamond earrings in the neck.

I have stolen the hen, but my god,
not for the diamonds.

In the attic, I read the registry from her funeral.
My God, I miss her—

Apartment J-82

With the taste
of good behavior

from another man's lips
still on my lips, I ate

the wedding cake topper
without you.

From the freezer
I pulled it from its box

and removed the bow—as if to
finally let loose my hair.

The sweet roses and figs
cut my throat.

Once we were
a fury of white feathers

around the room, unable
to wait for one another.

My wedding dress slumps
on the closet floor—

I am ready for home
now my marriage is gone

and my apartment is a grave
of dead birds.

The Poem for Evelyn

> *-She cannot be torn from the shell without dying*
> *Evelyn Scott* (1893-1963)

You wrote about women as shells
gliding across their little waters.

I am trapped
along the same skim of river—

the cervix that holds us in.

I wonder where you
were when you saw

the teapots, tables and pictures on walls—
did you feel the same steeples

like coffin nails
around you?

You and I have done our best
to die here.

Mixing with your ghost,
I have asked, too, to leave.

And I, too, have failed
to cut off the bruise from our inedible pears.

Why Death recalls more Lovers and Cats than the Moon (or why I am the lonely Cat Lady up talking to God at 4 a.m.)

Because: I am homesick for the stray cats
in the *piazza* where he broke the thin layer of

Christmas in my chest—then left like rain leaves
without any warning. Because: the tree blinks

some neon North Star off and on: off and on:
half-nun, half-whore, half-nun, half-whore.

Because: the moon looks like a broken bowl,
and hoping to mend to it, I tape feathers to the walls

so I can fly. Because: the new apartment is not
a launch pad, but a den of shadows. Because:

the last wish of the dying to not go alone is turning
its lips blue. Because: the feathers breathe up and back

when I try to crawl down from the ceiling emptying
like a great raging thunderstorm. Because: night sings

wildness into me, and I lie in the shadows of hungry cats
lying in the snow of feathers beating the floors.

Because: still only the loneliness of a sunrise
and the silence of walls answer in return.

Because:
I hope the cats don't starve.

Sometimes I Pack my Things and Leave

I sleep uneasy, startling from dreams,
and then blame the stars

against the panes of the windows
for waking me each night,

for urging another sleepless woman
to cut the locks of her hair

and turn the locks of her doors.
You'll rise, you said. *Afterward you'll rise*

from your darkness, and the two small children
growing like geese in your gray cloud,

will be urged on by those same stars
that keep you awake.

Acknowledgments—

"The Generation Dress" published by Big River Poetry
        Review
"Loneliness Came Inside My Home, Unpacked its
        Things" published by Words Dance
"Sometimes the Blood Goes Cold" published by
        THRUSH Poetry Journal
"After Jake's Funeral" published by The Penmen Review
"Dirt" published by Sow's Ear Poetry Review
"When Joe Proposed" published by The Exhibit
"Leftovers" published by Eunoia Review
"Gallup, New Mexico" published by The Dressing
        Room Poetry Journal
"Regret" published by Eclectica Magazine
"Married Women, and other degenerates" published by
        Connotation-Press
"Sometimes I Pack my Things and Leave" published by
        The Exhibit
"Between the silences there are sounds like panic"
        published by Vinyl Poetry
"Like the Black Hole Cartographer Who Went Hunting
        for Walnuts" published by Rogue Agent Journal
"Barriers" published by Kentucky Review

Special Thanks—

I would like to thank the following people who have provided amazing support along the way: Jennifer Givhan for being my dearest friend and mentor, Emily Graham & Holly Haimes who are my North, South, East & West, The Rooster Moans Poetry Cooperative where many of these poems began, The Blue Hou Press who have made this possible—especially Heather Minett for her constant encouragement and love, Andrea Spofford, Amy Wright, Barry Kitterman, The Lang & Lit Department at Austin Peay State University, and last but not least, Samuel Barber, for writing Adagio for Strings, Opus 11.

Stephanie Bryant Anderson is the founder of Red Paint Hill Publishing. She has worked also as editor with *Up the Staircase Quarterly*, Inkception Books, and she served on the Editorial Board for *The Manatee*, Southern New Hampshire University's literary journal. Nominated for Best of the Net, storySouth Million Writers Award, and twice for the Pushcart Prize, Stephanie is the mother to two amazing boys. Besides poetry she enjoys kickboxing and math.

CPSIA information can be obtained
at www.ICGtesting.com
Printed in the USA
FSOW04n1624020615
7525FS